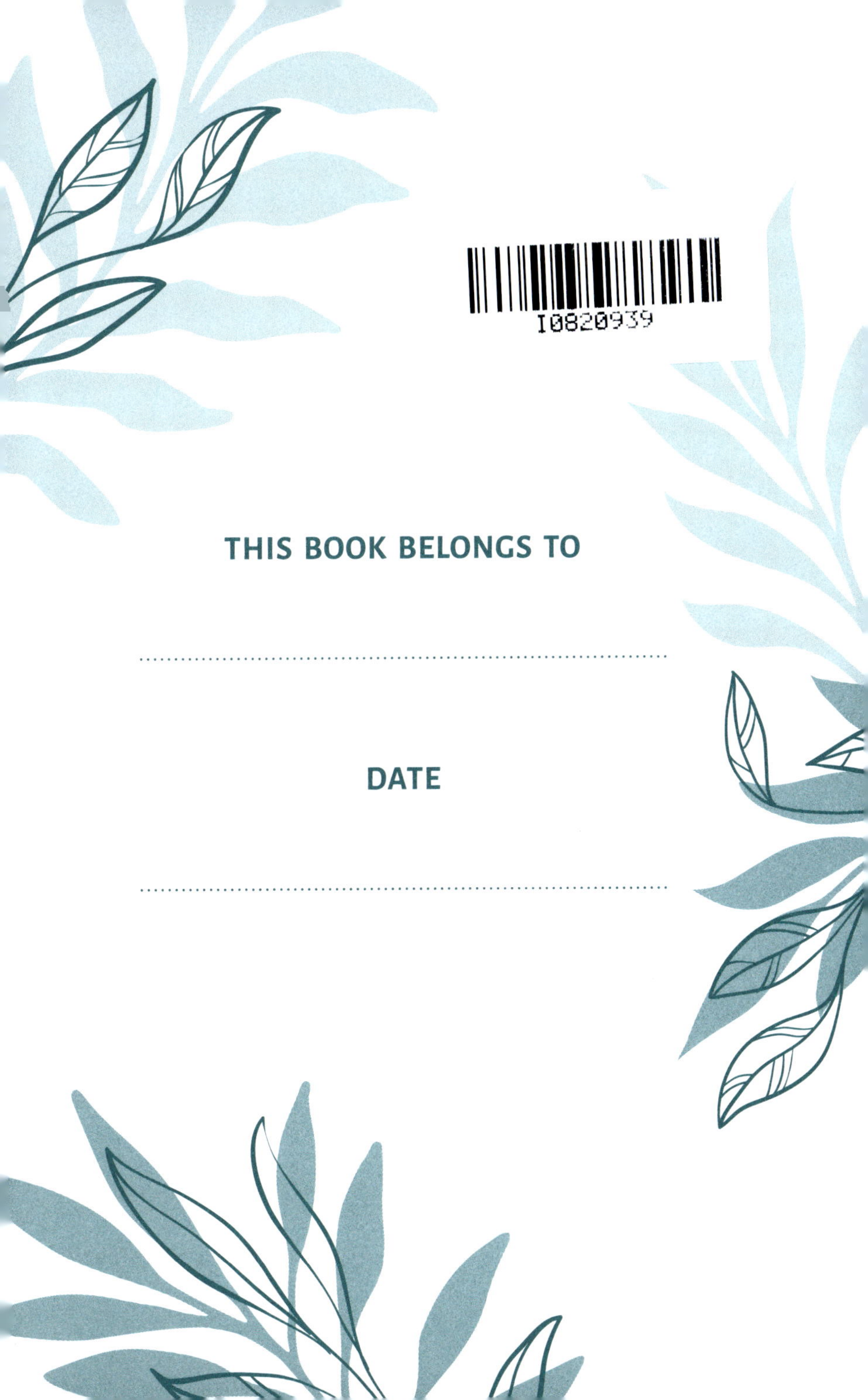

I0820939

THIS BOOK BELONGS TO

....

DATE

....

THE BIBLE STUDY COLLECTIVE

Verse Mapping Journal

A Visual Bible Study Guide

ISBN 979-8-89151-202-3

Published by Barbour Publishing, Inc., 1810 Barbour Drive, Uhrichsville, Ohio 44683, www.barbourbooks.com

Our mission is to inspire the world with the life-changing message of the Bible.

Printed in China.

INTRODUCTION

A BREAKTHROUGH APPROACH TO PERSONAL BIBLE STUDY.

Are you ready to go deeper than just reading your Bible? Barbour's popular Prayer Map notebooks have sold hundreds of thousands of copies, helping readers everywhere to visualize their prayer requests. Now, this *Verse Mapping Journal* does the same thing for the study of scripture.

A new facet of the Bible Study Collective series, this journal guides you to dig into scripture and unlock your understanding of God's Word. First, you'll be encouraged to select your own verse or verses for study—and if you don't know where to start, take a look at pages 10–13 for a list of impactful passages. Then, through the inductive method of Bible study, you'll observe, interpret, and apply the truths of scripture as you unpack what God's Word means to your life today. Whether you're just beginning to study scripture or you're a veteran verse mapper, this journal will help you discover

- connections within verses as you unravel the who, what, why, and how of scripture

AND

- the connections between those passages and your own life.

On the next few pages, you'll find a guide to verse mapping and a sample study to give you an idea of how the *Verse Mapping Journal* works. But you're welcome to adapt the process in whatever way works best for you. The important thing is that you're spending serious study time in God's Word.

Your personal Bible study may never be the same!

VERSE MAPPING STEP-BY-STEP:

HOW TO STUDY THE BIBLE IN A MORE MEANINGFUL WAY!

Grab your Bible and something to write with, and let's start mapping. Feel free to use colored pencils, pens, or markers if that aids your study. If you'd like to go deeper, bring along a concordance with Hebrew and Greek definitions, or look them up online.

1. **Verse:** Select and record your scripture, then write it in another translation as well.
2. **Notice:** Underline similar (or different) keywords in your translations. Note themes or questions you have as you first consider the verse.

   Bonus: Using a concordance, write the Greek or Hebrew definitions of your keywords here.

3. **Study:** Here is the inductive study method of observation. Without trying to explain anything, simply note the subjects—the whos and whats of the verse.
4. **Study:** Here is a second round of observation. Without trying to explain anything, simply note the actions in your scripture—the key verbs.
5. **Connect:** Now you begin interpretation. Connect the subjects and actions of steps 3 and 4. What does God seem to be saying through these connections?

   Bonus: Using a concordance, jot down other scripture references that relate to your study verse.

6. **Live It:** Now you're ready for application to your own life. What is God saying to *you*?
7. **Pray:** Write out your own request for God to use this study in a powerful way in your life.

The example study on the next two pages shows how all of these elements come together in the Verse Mapping process.

EXAMPLE VERSE MAPPING STUDY

1.

VERSE: What scripture am I exploring today?

In my favorite translation: Study to show yourself approved to God, a workman who does not need to be ashamed, rightly dividing the word of truth. 2 Timothy 2:15 SKJV

In another translation: Be diligent to present yourself to God as one approved, a worker who doesn't need to be ashamed, correctly teaching the word of truth. 2 Timothy 2:15 CSB

2.

NOTICE: What key words or themes immediately grab my attention? What questions come to mind?

God wants me to study His Word. There is work involved in understanding the "word of truth."

Bonus Word Study

Study—"to be diligent, strive, exert, oneself, make haste" Rightly dividing—"to cut straight"

3.

STUDY: Who is acting in this passage? What things are involved? What ideas are present?

- an implied "you". . . actually, ME
- God, and His "word of truth"
- a workman

4.

STUDY: What's going on in this verse? What action words do I see?

- study
- "show yourself approved"
- "does not need to be ashamed"
- dividing

5.

CONNECT: How do the actions in this verse connect with the people or things involved?

- as a reader of 2 Tim. 2:15, I am called to study "the word of truth"
- God will approve of those who study (and properly teach) His Word
- it takes "a workman" (or worker) to study God's Word—and the one who does has no reason for shame
- I am "dividing" God's Word—cutting it into pieces, cutting it straight—to properly understand
- there is a right way to do this—and apparently a wrong way

Bonus Cross Reference

I Thes. 2:4, 2 Pet. 1:10

6.

LIVE IT: What is God saying to *me* in this verse? What does this passage speak to my life right now?

- I am starting a journey of personal Bible study in pursuit of God's approval
- I don't want to be ashamed by a lack of knowledge—or effort
- I must commit myself to the job, since Bible students are called "workmen"
- I need to "rightly divide" God's Word in order to get (and share) its benefit. . . and I'll need the Author's input to do that!

7.

PRAY: How do I want God to work in me through this study?

Lord, I want to know You better by knowing Your Word more completely. Please guide my efforts in Bible study so that I can become more like You every day.

SUGGESTED SCRIPTURES FOR STUDY

Abiding in Christ .... John 15:4–5; 1 John 2:28–29

Abundance, Spiritual .... Psalm 36:7–9; John 10:9–10; 2 Corinthians 9:8

Acceptance by God .... Acts 10:34–35; Ephesians 1:5–6

Affliction .... 2 Corinthians 4:17–18; Hebrews 12:11

Anger .... Matthew 5:22; James 1:19–20

Anxiety .... Philippians 4:6–7; 1 Peter 5:6–7

Backsliding .... Luke 9:61–62; Galatians 4:8–10

Bible, the .... Matthew 5:18; 2 Timothy 3:16–17

Blessing of God .... Psalm 65:9; Malachi 3:10; Luke 11:13

Burdens .... 2 Corinthians 5:4; Galatians 6:1–2

Calling, Christian .... 1 Thessalonians 2:11–12; 1 Peter 5:10

Cleansing, Spiritual .... 2 Corinthians 7:1; James 4:7–8; 1 John 3:2–3

Conscience .... 2 Corinthians 1:12; 1 Peter 3:15–16

Contentment .... Philippians 4:11–13; Hebrews 13:5

Death .... Psalm 23:4; Romans 14:8; Hebrews 9:27–28

Discipleship .... Matthew 16:24–25; Luke 14:31–33; John 15:7–8

Doubt .... Matthew 14:29–31; Mark 11:23–24

Encouragement .... Isaiah 41:13–14; Matthew 14:26–27

Enemies .... Psalm 18:47–48; Matthew 5:43–45; Luke 23:33–34

Eternal Life .... John 3:16–17; John 17:1–3; Galatians 6:7–8

Faithfulness .... Deuteronomy 7:9; Luke 19:17; Revelation 2:10

Fear .... Proverbs 29:25; Isaiah 12:2; Matthew 10:29–31

Forgiveness .... Matthew 6:14–15; 1 John 1:9–10

Fruit, Spiritual .... Galatians 5:22–23; Ephesians 5:8–10; Philippians 1:9–11

Grace .... Romans 5:15; 2 Corinthians 12:9; 1 Timothy 1:12–13

Gratitude .... Psalm 100:4–5; Colossians 3:15–16; Hebrews 13:15–16

Holiness .... Leviticus 11:44–45; Isaiah 6:1–3; 1 Peter 3:10–12

Hope .... Romans 8:23–24; Colossians 1:3–5

Image of God .... Genesis 1:26–27; James 3:9–10

Influences .... Matthew 5:14–16; Hebrews 11:4

Joy .... Psalm 16:11; Romans 14:7–8; 1 Peter 4:12–13

Judging .... Matthew 7:1–2; Matthew 7:3–5

Kindness .... Romans 12:9–10; Ephesians 4:31–32; Colossians 3:12–13

Knowledge .... Proverbs 2:3–5; John 7:16–17

Loneliness .... Psalm 68:5–6; John 16:32–33

Love, God's .... Jeremiah 31:3; Romans 5:7–8; Ephesians 2:4–5

Mercy.................. Lamentations 3:22–24; Luke 6:35–36; Titus 3:4–5

Miracles...John 20:30–31

Obedience to God........................ 1 Samuel 15:22; Matthew 7:21–23; James 1:25

Peace.................John 14:25–27; Romans 8:5–6; Colossians 3:15–16

Persecution...............Luke 11:9–10; Luke 21:12; 2 Timothy 3:12–13

Prayer..........................2 Chronicles 7:14; Luke 18:1; James 5:13–15; James 5:16

Rewards, Spiritual................................ Genesis 15:1; Matthew 6:3–4; Revelation 22:12–13

Righteousness.........................Hosea 10:12; 1 Corinthians 15:33–34; Ephesians 6:14–16

Salvation.....................Acts 4:11–12; Romans 6:23; Ephesians 2:8–9; 2 Peter 3:9

Satan.................... John 8:44; 2 Corinthians 11:14–15; 1 Peter 5:8–9

Self-Control....................................Proverbs 16:32; Romans 6:12–13; 2 Peter 1:5–7

Sin...................................... Isaiah 53:6; Isaiah 64:6; Romans 3:21–23; Ephesians 4:22–24

Speech...Titus 3:1–2; James 1:26; James 3:6

Suffering.......................................Matthew 19:29; Romans 8:16–17; Hebrews 11:24–25

Trials..2 Corinthians 8:1–2; James 1:2–3; 2 Peter 2:7–9

Trust in God..............Psalm 37:3–4; Proverbs 3:5–6; Isaiah 26:3–4; Habakkuk 3:17–18

Victory, Spiritual..................................Romans 8:35–37; 1 John 5:4; Revelation 3:21

Walk of Faith.. Romans 6:4; Ephesians 5:15–17; 1 John 1:6–7

Wisdom..................Proverbs 4:6–7; 1 Corinthians 1:25; James 1:5–6; James 3:17

Womanhood................................ Proverbs 31:10–11; Proverbs 31:30; 1 Peter 3:1–2

Zeal...............................John 2:16–17; 1 Corinthians 10:31; Titus 2:14

DATE:

1. **VERSE:** What scripture am I exploring today?

In my favorite translation:

In another translation:

2. **NOTICE:** What key words or themes immediately grab my attention? What questions come to mind?

Bonus Word Study

3. **STUDY:** Who is acting in this passage? What things are involved? What ideas are present?

4. **STUDY:** What's going on in this verse? What action words do I see?

5.

CONNECT: How do the actions in this verse connect with the people or things involved?

Bonus Cross Reference

6.

LIVE IT: What is God saying to *me* in this verse? What does this passage speak to my life right now?

7.

PRAY: How do I want God to work in me through this study?

DATE:

1. **VERSE:** What scripture am I exploring today?

In my favorite translation:

In another translation:

2. **NOTICE:** What key words or themes immediately grab my attention? What questions come to mind?

Bonus Word Study

3. **STUDY:** Who is acting in this passage? What things are involved? What ideas are present?

4. **STUDY:** What's going on in this verse? What action words do I see?

5.

CONNECT: How do the actions in this verse connect with the people or things involved?

Bonus Cross Reference

6.

LIVE IT: What is God saying to *me* in this verse? What does this passage speak to my life right now?

7.

PRAY: How do I want God to work in me through this study?

DATE:

1.

VERSE: What scripture am I exploring today?

In my favorite translation:

In another translation:

2.

NOTICE: What key words or themes immediately grab my attention? What questions come to mind?

Bonus Word Study

3.

STUDY: Who is acting in this passage? What things are involved? What ideas are present?

4.

STUDY: What's going on in this verse? What action words do I see?

5.

CONNECT: How do the actions in this verse connect with the people or things involved?

Bonus Cross Reference

6.

LIVE IT: What is God saying to *me* in this verse? What does this passage speak to my life right now?

7.

PRAY: How do I want God to work in me through this study?

DATE:

1.

VERSE: What scripture am I exploring today?

In my favorite translation:

In another translation:

2.

NOTICE: What key words or themes immediately grab my attention? What questions come to mind?

Bonus Word Study

3.

STUDY: Who is acting in this passage? What things are involved? What ideas are present?

4.

STUDY: What's going on in this verse? What action words do I see?

5.

CONNECT: How do the actions in this verse connect with the people or things involved?

Bonus Cross Reference

6.

LIVE IT: What is God saying to *me* in this verse? What does this passage speak to my life right now?

7.

PRAY: How do I want God to work in me through this study?

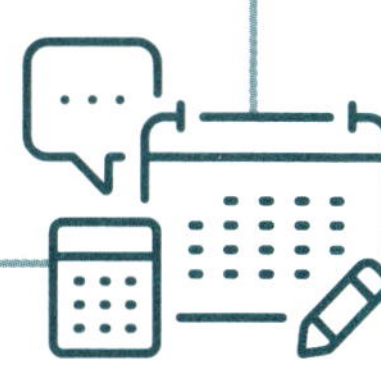

DATE:

1. **VERSE:** What scripture am I exploring today?

In my favorite translation:

In another translation:

2. **NOTICE:** What key words or themes immediately grab my attention? What questions come to mind?

Bonus Word Study

3. **STUDY:** Who is acting in this passage? What things are involved? What ideas are present?

4. **STUDY:** What's going on in this verse? What action words do I see?

5.

CONNECT: How do the actions in this verse connect with the people or things involved?

Bonus Cross Reference

6.

LIVE IT: What is God saying to *me* in this verse? What does this passage speak to my life right now?

7.

PRAY: How do I want God to work in me through this study?

DATE:

1.

VERSE: What scripture am I exploring today?

In my favorite translation:

In another translation:

2.

NOTICE: What key words or themes immediately grab my attention? What questions come to mind?

Bonus Word Study

3.

STUDY: Who is acting in this passage? What things are involved? What ideas are present?

4.

STUDY: What's going on in this verse? What action words do I see?

5.

CONNECT: How do the actions in this verse connect with the people or things involved?

Bonus Cross Reference

6.

LIVE IT: What is God saying to *me* in this verse? What does this passage speak to my life right now?

7.

PRAY: How do I want God to work in me through this study?

DATE:

1\. **VERSE:** What scripture am I exploring today?

In my favorite translation:

In another translation:

2\. **NOTICE:** What key words or themes immediately grab my attention? What questions come to mind?

Bonus Word Study

3\. **STUDY:** Who is acting in this passage? What things are involved? What ideas are present?

4\. **STUDY:** What's going on in this verse? What action words do I see?

5.

CONNECT: How do the actions in this verse connect with the people or things involved?

Bonus Cross Reference

6.

LIVE IT: What is God saying to *me* in this verse? What does this passage speak to my life right now?

7.

PRAY: How do I want God to work in me through this study?

DATE:

1. **VERSE:** What scripture am I exploring today?

In my favorite translation:

In another translation:

2. **NOTICE:** What key words or themes immediately grab my attention? What questions come to mind?

Bonus Word Study

3. **STUDY:** Who is acting in this passage? What things are involved? What ideas are present?

4. **STUDY:** What's going on in this verse? What action words do I see?

5.

CONNECT: How do the actions in this verse connect with the people or things involved?

Bonus Cross Reference

6.

LIVE IT: What is God saying to *me* in this verse? What does this passage speak to my life right now?

7.

PRAY: How do I want God to work in me through this study?

DATE:

1. **VERSE:** What scripture am I exploring today?

In my favorite translation:

In another translation:

2. **NOTICE:** What key words or themes immediately grab my attention? What questions come to mind?

Bonus Word Study

3. **STUDY:** Who is acting in this passage? What things are involved? What ideas are present?

4. **STUDY:** What's going on in this verse? What action words do I see?

5.

CONNECT: How do the actions in this verse connect with the people or things involved?

Bonus Cross Reference

6.

LIVE IT: What is God saying to *me* in this verse? What does this passage speak to my life right now?

7.

PRAY: How do I want God to work in me through this study?

DATE:

1. **VERSE:** What scripture am I exploring today?

In my favorite translation:

In another translation:

2. **NOTICE:** What key words or themes immediately grab my attention? What questions come to mind?

Bonus Word Study

3. **STUDY:** Who is acting in this passage? What things are involved? What ideas are present?

4. **STUDY:** What's going on in this verse? What action words do I see?

5.

CONNECT: How do the actions in this verse connect with the people or things involved?

Bonus Cross Reference

6.

LIVE IT: What is God saying to *me* in this verse? What does this passage speak to my life right now?

7.

PRAY: How do I want God to work in me through this study?

DATE:

1\. **VERSE:** What scripture am I exploring today?

In my favorite translation:

In another translation:

2\. **NOTICE:** What key words or themes immediately grab my attention? What questions come to mind?

Bonus Word Study

3\. **STUDY:** Who is acting in this passage? What things are involved? What ideas are present?

4\. **STUDY:** What's going on in this verse? What action words do I see?

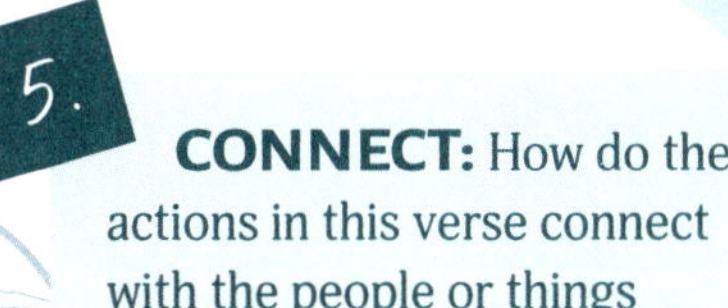

5.

CONNECT: How do the actions in this verse connect with the people or things involved?

Bonus Cross Reference

6.

LIVE IT: What is God saying to *me* in this verse? What does this passage speak to my life right now?

7.

PRAY: How do I want God to work in me through this study?

DATE:

1\.

VERSE: What scripture am I exploring today?

In my favorite translation:

In another translation:

2\.

NOTICE: What key words or themes immediately grab my attention? What questions come to mind?

Bonus Word Study

3\.

STUDY: Who is acting in this passage? What things are involved? What ideas are present?

4\.

STUDY: What's going on in this verse? What action words do I see?

5.

CONNECT: How do the actions in this verse connect with the people or things involved?

Bonus Cross Reference

6.

LIVE IT: What is God saying to *me* in this verse? What does this passage speak to my life right now?

7.

PRAY: How do I want God to work in me through this study?

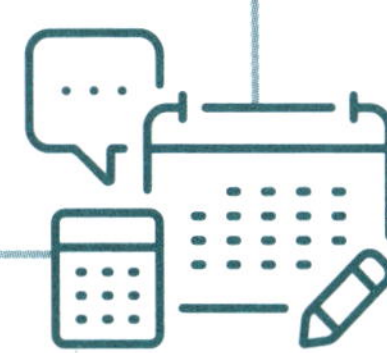

DATE:

1. **VERSE:** What scripture am I exploring today?

In my favorite translation:

In another translation:

2. **NOTICE:** What key words or themes immediately grab my attention? What questions come to mind?

Bonus Word Study

3. **STUDY:** Who is acting in this passage? What things are involved? What ideas are present?

4. **STUDY:** What's going on in this verse? What action words do I see?

5.

CONNECT: How do the actions in this verse connect with the people or things involved?

Bonus Cross Reference

6.

LIVE IT: What is God saying to *me* in this verse? What does this passage speak to my life right now?

7.

PRAY: How do I want God to work in me through this study?

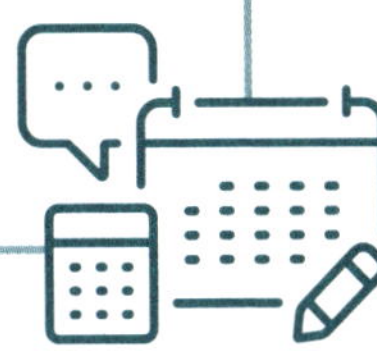

DATE:

1.

VERSE: What scripture am I exploring today?

In my favorite translation:

In another translation:

2.

NOTICE: What key words or themes immediately grab my attention? What questions come to mind?

Bonus Word Study

3.

STUDY: Who is acting in this passage? What things are involved? What ideas are present?

4.

STUDY: What's going on in this verse? What action words do I see?

5.

CONNECT: How do the actions in this verse connect with the people or things involved?

Bonus Cross Reference

6.

LIVE IT: What is God saying to *me* in this verse? What does this passage speak to my life right now?

7.

PRAY: How do I want God to work in me through this study?

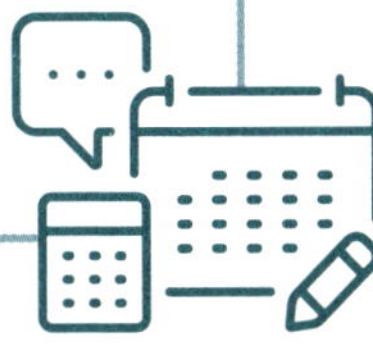

DATE:

1. **VERSE:** What scripture am I exploring today?

In my favorite translation:

In another translation:

2. **NOTICE:** What key words or themes immediately grab my attention? What questions come to mind?

Bonus Word Study

3. **STUDY:** Who is acting in this passage? What things are involved? What ideas are present?

4. **STUDY:** What's going on in this verse? What action words do I see?

5.

CONNECT: How do the actions in this verse connect with the people or things involved?

Bonus Cross Reference

6.

LIVE IT: What is God saying to *me* in this verse? What does this passage speak to my life right now?

7.

PRAY: How do I want God to work in me through this study?

DATE:

1. **VERSE:** What scripture am I exploring today?

In my favorite translation:

In another translation:

2. **NOTICE:** What key words or themes immediately grab my attention? What questions come to mind?

Bonus Word Study

3. **STUDY:** Who is acting in this passage? What things are involved? What ideas are present?

4. **STUDY:** What's going on in this verse? What action words do I see?

5.

CONNECT: How do the actions in this verse connect with the people or things involved?

Bonus Cross Reference

6.

LIVE IT: What is God saying to *me* in this verse? What does this passage speak to my life right now?

7.

PRAY: How do I want God to work in me through this study?

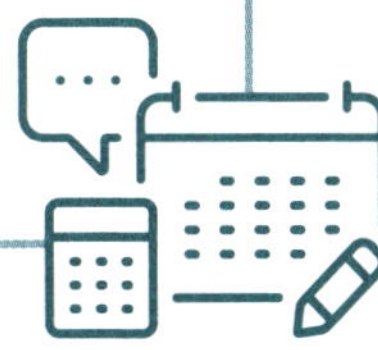

DATE:

1. **VERSE:** What scripture am I exploring today?

In my favorite translation:

In another translation:

2. **NOTICE:** What key words or themes immediately grab my attention? What questions come to mind?

Bonus Word Study

3. **STUDY:** Who is acting in this passage? What things are involved? What ideas are present?

4. **STUDY:** What's going on in this verse? What action words do I see?

5.

CONNECT: How do the actions in this verse connect with the people or things involved?

Bonus Cross Reference

6.

LIVE IT: What is God saying to *me* in this verse? What does this passage speak to my life right now?

7.

PRAY: How do I want God to work in me through this study?

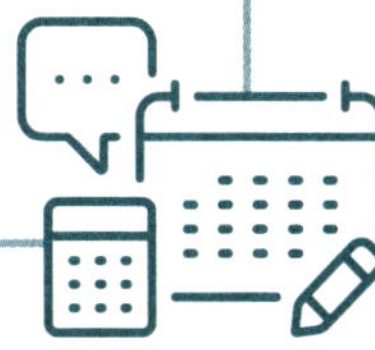

DATE:

1.

VERSE: What scripture am I exploring today?

In my favorite translation:

In another translation:

2.

NOTICE: What key words or themes immediately grab my attention? What questions come to mind?

Bonus Word Study

3.

STUDY: Who is acting in this passage? What things are involved? What ideas are present?

4.

STUDY: What's going on in this verse? What action words do I see?

5.

CONNECT: How do the actions in this verse connect with the people or things involved?

Bonus Cross Reference

6.

LIVE IT: What is God saying to *me* in this verse? What does this passage speak to my life right now?

7.

PRAY: How do I want God to work in me through this study?

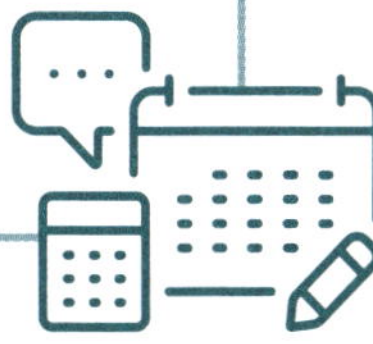

DATE:

1. **VERSE:** What scripture am I exploring today?

In my favorite translation:

In another translation:

2. **NOTICE:** What key words or themes immediately grab my attention? What questions come to mind?

Bonus Word Study

3. **STUDY:** Who is acting in this passage? What things are involved? What ideas are present?

4. **STUDY:** What's going on in this verse? What action words do I see?

5.

CONNECT: How do the actions in this verse connect with the people or things involved?

Bonus Cross Reference

6.

LIVE IT: What is God saying to *me* in this verse? What does this passage speak to my life right now?

7.

PRAY: How do I want God to work in me through this study?

DATE:

1. **VERSE:** What scripture am I exploring today?

In my favorite translation:

In another translation:

2. **NOTICE:** What key words or themes immediately grab my attention? What questions come to mind?

Bonus Word Study

3. **STUDY:** Who is acting in this passage? What things are involved? What ideas are present?

4. **STUDY:** What's going on in this verse? What action words do I see?

5.

CONNECT: How do the actions in this verse connect with the people or things involved?

Bonus Cross Reference

6.

LIVE IT: What is God saying to *me* in this verse? What does this passage speak to my life right now?

7.

PRAY: How do I want God to work in me through this study?

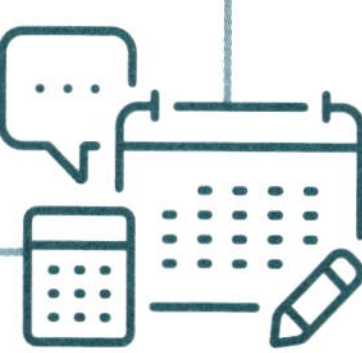

DATE:

1.

VERSE: What scripture am I exploring today?

In my favorite translation:

In another translation:

2.

NOTICE: What key words or themes immediately grab my attention? What questions come to mind?

Bonus Word Study

3.

STUDY: Who is acting in this passage? What things are involved? What ideas are present?

4.

STUDY: What's going on in this verse? What action words do I see?

5.

CONNECT: How do the actions in this verse connect with the people or things involved?

Bonus Cross Reference

6.

LIVE IT: What is God saying to *me* in this verse? What does this passage speak to my life right now?

7.

PRAY: How do I want God to work in me through this study?

DATE:

1. **VERSE:** What scripture am I exploring today?

In my favorite translation:

In another translation:

2. **NOTICE:** What key words or themes immediately grab my attention? What questions come to mind?

Bonus Word Study

3. **STUDY:** Who is acting in this passage? What things are involved? What ideas are present?

4. **STUDY:** What's going on in this verse? What action words do I see?

5.

CONNECT: How do the actions in this verse connect with the people or things involved?

Bonus Cross Reference

6.

LIVE IT: What is God saying to *me* in this verse? What does this passage speak to my life right now?

7.

PRAY: How do I want God to work in me through this study?

DATE:

1. **VERSE:** What scripture am I exploring today?

In my favorite translation:

In another translation:

2. **NOTICE:** What key words or themes immediately grab my attention? What questions come to mind?

Bonus Word Study

3. **STUDY:** Who is acting in this passage? What things are involved? What ideas are present?

4. **STUDY:** What's going on in this verse? What action words do I see?

5.

CONNECT: How do the actions in this verse connect with the people or things involved?

Bonus Cross Reference

6.

LIVE IT: What is God saying to *me* in this verse? What does this passage speak to my life right now?

7.

PRAY: How do I want God to work in me through this study?

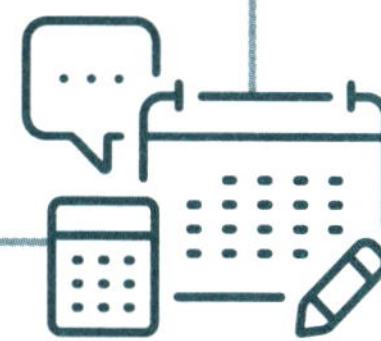

DATE:

1. **VERSE:** What scripture am I exploring today?

In my favorite translation:

In another translation:

2. **NOTICE:** What key words or themes immediately grab my attention? What questions come to mind?

Bonus Word Study

3. **STUDY:** Who is acting in this passage? What things are involved? What ideas are present?

4. **STUDY:** What's going on in this verse? What action words do I see?

5.

CONNECT: How do the actions in this verse connect with the people or things involved?

Bonus Cross Reference

6.

LIVE IT: What is God saying to *me* in this verse? What does this passage speak to my life right now?

7.

PRAY: How do I want God to work in me through this study?

DATE:

1.

VERSE: What scripture am I exploring today?

In my favorite translation:

In another translation:

2.

NOTICE: What key words or themes immediately grab my attention? What questions come to mind?

Bonus Word Study

3.

STUDY: Who is acting in this passage? What things are involved? What ideas are present?

4.

STUDY: What's going on in this verse? What action words do I see?

5\. **CONNECT:** How do the actions in this verse connect with the people or things involved?

Bonus Cross Reference

6\. **LIVE IT:** What is God saying to *me* in this verse? What does this passage speak to my life right now?

7\. **PRAY:** How do I want God to work in me through this study?

DATE:

1. **VERSE:** What scripture am I exploring today?

In my favorite translation:

In another translation:

2. **NOTICE:** What key words or themes immediately grab my attention? What questions come to mind?

Bonus Word Study

3. **STUDY:** Who is acting in this passage? What things are involved? What ideas are present?

4. **STUDY:** What's going on in this verse? What action words do I see?

5.

CONNECT: How do the actions in this verse connect with the people or things involved?

Bonus Cross Reference

6.

LIVE IT: What is God saying to *me* in this verse? What does this passage speak to my life right now?

7.

PRAY: How do I want God to work in me through this study?

DATE:

1. **VERSE:** What scripture am I exploring today?

In my favorite translation:

In another translation:

2. **NOTICE:** What key words or themes immediately grab my attention? What questions come to mind?

Bonus Word Study

3. **STUDY:** Who is acting in this passage? What things are involved? What ideas are present?

4. **STUDY:** What's going on in this verse? What action words do I see?

5.

CONNECT: How do the actions in this verse connect with the people or things involved?

Bonus Cross Reference

6.

LIVE IT: What is God saying to *me* in this verse? What does this passage speak to my life right now?

7.

PRAY: How do I want God to work in me through this study?

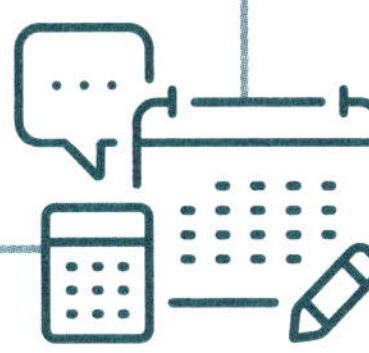

DATE:

1.

VERSE: What scripture am I exploring today?

In my favorite translation:

In another translation:

2.

NOTICE: What key words or themes immediately grab my attention? What questions come to mind?

Bonus Word Study

3.

STUDY: Who is acting in this passage? What things are involved? What ideas are present?

4.

STUDY: What's going on in this verse? What action words do I see?

5.

CONNECT: How do the actions in this verse connect with the people or things involved?

Bonus Cross Reference

6.

LIVE IT: What is God saying to *me* in this verse? What does this passage speak to my life right now?

7.

PRAY: How do I want God to work in me through this study?

DATE:

1.

VERSE: What scripture am I exploring today?

In my favorite translation:

In another translation:

2.

NOTICE: What key words or themes immediately grab my attention? What questions come to mind?

Bonus Word Study

3.

STUDY: Who is acting in this passage? What things are involved? What ideas are present?

4.

STUDY: What's going on in this verse? What action words do I see?

5.

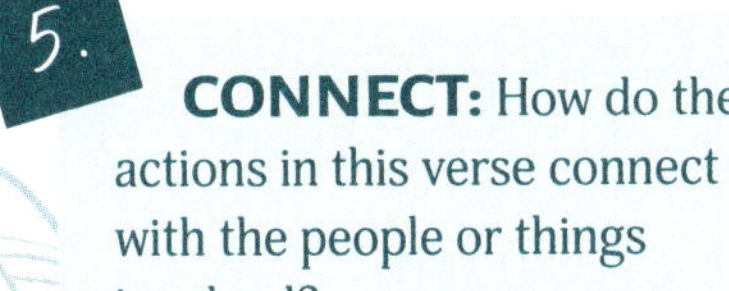

CONNECT: How do the actions in this verse connect with the people or things involved?

Bonus Cross Reference

6.

LIVE IT: What is God saying to *me* in this verse? What does this passage speak to my life right now?

7.

PRAY: How do I want God to work in me through this study?

DATE:

1.

VERSE: What scripture am I exploring today?

In my favorite translation:

In another translation:

2.

NOTICE: What key words or themes immediately grab my attention? What questions come to mind?

Bonus Word Study

3.

STUDY: Who is acting in this passage? What things are involved? What ideas are present?

4.

STUDY: What's going on in this verse? What action words do I see?

5.

CONNECT: How do the actions in this verse connect with the people or things involved?

Bonus Cross Reference

6.

LIVE IT: What is God saying to *me* in this verse? What does this passage speak to my life right now?

7.

PRAY: How do I want God to work in me through this study?

DATE:

1. **VERSE:** What scripture am I exploring today?

In my favorite translation:

In another translation:

2. **NOTICE:** What key words or themes immediately grab my attention? What questions come to mind?

Bonus Word Study

3. **STUDY:** Who is acting in this passage? What things are involved? What ideas are present?

4. **STUDY:** What's going on in this verse? What action words do I see?

5.

CONNECT: How do the actions in this verse connect with the people or things involved?

Bonus Cross Reference

6.

LIVE IT: What is God saying to *me* in this verse? What does this passage speak to my life right now?

7.

PRAY: How do I want God to work in me through this study?

DATE:

1. **VERSE:** What scripture am I exploring today?

In my favorite translation:

In another translation:

2. **NOTICE:** What key words or themes immediately grab my attention? What questions come to mind?

Bonus Word Study

3. **STUDY:** Who is acting in this passage? What things are involved? What ideas are present?

4. **STUDY:** What's going on in this verse? What action words do I see?

5.

CONNECT: How do the actions in this verse connect with the people or things involved?

Bonus Cross Reference

6.

LIVE IT: What is God saying to *me* in this verse? What does this passage speak to my life right now?

7.

PRAY: How do I want God to work in me through this study?

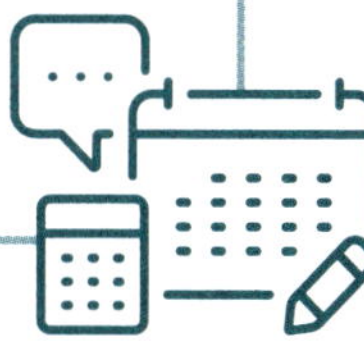

DATE:

1.

VERSE: What scripture am I exploring today?

In my favorite translation:

In another translation:

2.

NOTICE: What key words or themes immediately grab my attention? What questions come to mind?

Bonus Word Study

3.

STUDY: Who is acting in this passage? What things are involved? What ideas are present?

4.

STUDY: What's going on in this verse? What action words do I see?

5.

CONNECT: How do the actions in this verse connect with the people or things involved?

Bonus Cross Reference

6.

LIVE IT: What is God saying to *me* in this verse? What does this passage speak to my life right now?

7.

PRAY: How do I want God to work in me through this study?

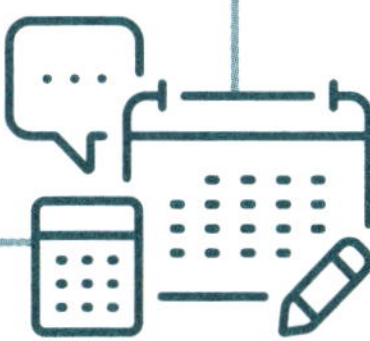

DATE:

1\. **VERSE:** What scripture am I exploring today?

In my favorite translation:

In another translation:

2\. **NOTICE:** What key words or themes immediately grab my attention? What questions come to mind?

Bonus Word Study

3\. **STUDY:** Who is acting in this passage? What things are involved? What ideas are present?

4\. **STUDY:** What's going on in this verse? What action words do I see?

5.

CONNECT: How do the actions in this verse connect with the people or things involved?

Bonus Cross Reference

6.

LIVE IT: What is God saying to *me* in this verse? What does this passage speak to my life right now?

7.

PRAY: How do I want God to work in me through this study?

DATE:

1. **VERSE:** What scripture am I exploring today?

In my favorite translation:

In another translation:

2. **NOTICE:** What key words or themes immediately grab my attention? What questions come to mind?

Bonus Word Study

3. **STUDY:** Who is acting in this passage? What things are involved? What ideas are present?

4. **STUDY:** What's going on in this verse? What action words do I see?

5.

CONNECT: How do the actions in this verse connect with the people or things involved?

Bonus Cross Reference

6.

LIVE IT: What is God saying to *me* in this verse? What does this passage speak to my life right now?

7.

PRAY: How do I want God to work in me through this study?

DATE:

1. **VERSE:** What scripture am I exploring today?

In my favorite translation:

In another translation:

2. **NOTICE:** What key words or themes immediately grab my attention? What questions come to mind?

Bonus Word Study

3. **STUDY:** Who is acting in this passage? What things are involved? What ideas are present?

4. **STUDY:** What's going on in this verse? What action words do I see?

5.

CONNECT: How do the actions in this verse connect with the people or things involved?

Bonus Cross Reference

6.

LIVE IT: What is God saying to *me* in this verse? What does this passage speak to my life right now?

7.

PRAY: How do I want God to work in me through this study?

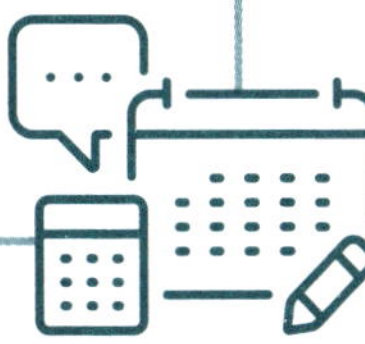

DATE:

1. **VERSE:** What scripture am I exploring today?

In my favorite translation:

In another translation:

2. **NOTICE:** What key words or themes immediately grab my attention? What questions come to mind?

Bonus Word Study

3. **STUDY:** Who is acting in this passage? What things are involved? What ideas are present?

4. **STUDY:** What's going on in this verse? What action words do I see?

5.

CONNECT: How do the actions in this verse connect with the people or things involved?

Bonus Cross Reference

6.

LIVE IT: What is God saying to *me* in this verse? What does this passage speak to my life right now?

7.

PRAY: How do I want God to work in me through this study?

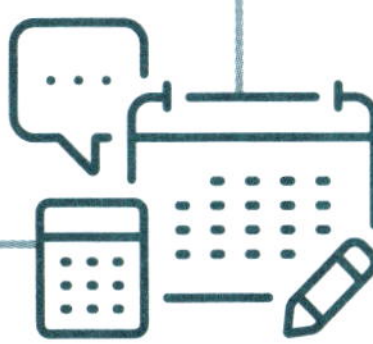

DATE:

1. **VERSE:** What scripture am I exploring today?

In my favorite translation:

In another translation:

2. **NOTICE:** What key words or themes immediately grab my attention? What questions come to mind?

Bonus Word Study

3. **STUDY:** Who is acting in this passage? What things are involved? What ideas are present?

4. **STUDY:** What's going on in this verse? What action words do I see?

5.

CONNECT: How do the actions in this verse connect with the people or things involved?

Bonus Cross Reference

6.

LIVE IT: What is God saying to *me* in this verse? What does this passage speak to my life right now?

7.

PRAY: How do I want God to work in me through this study?

DATE:

1. **VERSE:** What scripture am I exploring today?

In my favorite translation:

In another translation:

2. **NOTICE:** What key words or themes immediately grab my attention? What questions come to mind?

Bonus Word Study

3. **STUDY:** Who is acting in this passage? What things are involved? What ideas are present?

4. **STUDY:** What's going on in this verse? What action words do I see?

5.

CONNECT: How do the actions in this verse connect with the people or things involved?

Bonus Cross Reference

6.

LIVE IT: What is God saying to *me* in this verse? What does this passage speak to my life right now?

7.

PRAY: How do I want God to work in me through this study?

DATE:

1\. **VERSE:** What scripture am I exploring today?

In my favorite translation:

In another translation:

2\. **NOTICE:** What key words or themes immediately grab my attention? What questions come to mind?

Bonus Word Study

3\. **STUDY:** Who is acting in this passage? What things are involved? What ideas are present?

4\. **STUDY:** What's going on in this verse? What action words do I see?

CONNECT: How do the actions in this verse connect with the people or things involved?

Bonus Cross Reference

LIVE IT: What is God saying to *me* in this verse? What does this passage speak to my life right now?

PRAY: How do I want God to work in me through this study?

DATE:

1\. **VERSE:** What scripture am I exploring today?

In my favorite translation:

In another translation:

2\. **NOTICE:** What key words or themes immediately grab my attention? What questions come to mind?

Bonus Word Study

3\. **STUDY:** Who is acting in this passage? What things are involved? What ideas are present?

4\. **STUDY:** What's going on in this verse? What action words do I see?

5.

CONNECT: How do the actions in this verse connect with the people or things involved?

Bonus Cross Reference

6.

LIVE IT: What is God saying to *me* in this verse? What does this passage speak to my life right now?

7.

PRAY: How do I want God to work in me through this study?

DATE:

1. **VERSE:** What scripture am I exploring today?

In my favorite translation:

In another translation:

2. **NOTICE:** What key words or themes immediately grab my attention? What questions come to mind?

Bonus Word Study

3. **STUDY:** Who is acting in this passage? What things are involved? What ideas are present?

4. **STUDY:** What's going on in this verse? What action words do I see?

5.

CONNECT: How do the actions in this verse connect with the people or things involved?

Bonus Cross Reference

6.

LIVE IT: What is God saying to *me* in this verse? What does this passage speak to my life right now?

7.

PRAY: How do I want God to work in me through this study?

DATE:

1. **VERSE:** What scripture am I exploring today?

In my favorite translation:

In another translation:

2. **NOTICE:** What key words or themes immediately grab my attention? What questions come to mind?

Bonus Word Study

3. **STUDY:** Who is acting in this passage? What things are involved? What ideas are present?

4. **STUDY:** What's going on in this verse? What action words do I see?

5.

CONNECT: How do the actions in this verse connect with the people or things involved?

Bonus Cross Reference

6.

LIVE IT: What is God saying to *me* in this verse? What does this passage speak to my life right now?

7.

PRAY: How do I want God to work in me through this study?

DATE:

1. **VERSE:** What scripture am I exploring today?

In my favorite translation:

In another translation:

2. **NOTICE:** What key words or themes immediately grab my attention? What questions come to mind?

Bonus Word Study

3. **STUDY:** Who is acting in this passage? What things are involved? What ideas are present?

4. **STUDY:** What's going on in this verse? What action words do I see?

5.

CONNECT: How do the actions in this verse connect with the people or things involved?

Bonus Cross Reference

6.

LIVE IT: What is God saying to *me* in this verse? What does this passage speak to my life right now?

7.

PRAY: How do I want God to work in me through this study?

DATE:

1. **VERSE:** What scripture am I exploring today?

In my favorite translation:

In another translation:

2. **NOTICE:** What key words or themes immediately grab my attention? What questions come to mind?

Bonus Word Study

3. **STUDY:** Who is acting in this passage? What things are involved? What ideas are present?

4. **STUDY:** What's going on in this verse? What action words do I see?

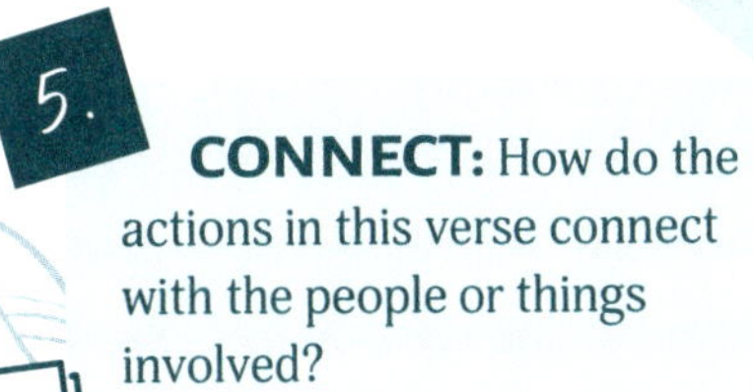

5.

CONNECT: How do the actions in this verse connect with the people or things involved?

Bonus Cross Reference

6.

LIVE IT: What is God saying to *me* in this verse? What does this passage speak to my life right now?

7.

PRAY: How do I want God to work in me through this study?

DATE:

1\. **VERSE:** What scripture am I exploring today?

In my favorite translation:

In another translation:

2\. **NOTICE:** What key words or themes immediately grab my attention? What questions come to mind?

Bonus Word Study

3\. **STUDY:** Who is acting in this passage? What things are involved? What ideas are present?

4\. **STUDY:** What's going on in this verse? What action words do I see?

5.

CONNECT: How do the actions in this verse connect with the people or things involved?

Bonus Cross Reference

6.

LIVE IT: What is God saying to *me* in this verse? What does this passage speak to my life right now?

7.

PRAY: How do I want God to work in me through this study?

DATE:

1. **VERSE:** What scripture am I exploring today?

In my favorite translation:

In another translation:

2. **NOTICE:** What key words or themes immediately grab my attention? What questions come to mind?

Bonus Word Study

3. **STUDY:** Who is acting in this passage? What things are involved? What ideas are present?

4. **STUDY:** What's going on in this verse? What action words do I see?

5.

CONNECT: How do the actions in this verse connect with the people or things involved?

Bonus Cross Reference

6.

LIVE IT: What is God saying to *me* in this verse? What does this passage speak to my life right now?

7.

PRAY: How do I want God to work in me through this study?

DATE:

1.

VERSE: What scripture am I exploring today?

In my favorite translation:

In another translation:

2.

NOTICE: What key words or themes immediately grab my attention? What questions come to mind?

Bonus Word Study

3.

STUDY: Who is acting in this passage? What things are involved? What ideas are present?

4.

STUDY: What's going on in this verse? What action words do I see?

5.

CONNECT: How do the actions in this verse connect with the people or things involved?

Bonus Cross Reference

6.

LIVE IT: What is God saying to *me* in this verse? What does this passage speak to my life right now?

7.

PRAY: How do I want God to work in me through this study?

DATE:

1. **VERSE:** What scripture am I exploring today?

In my favorite translation:

In another translation:

2. **NOTICE:** What key words or themes immediately grab my attention? What questions come to mind?

Bonus Word Study

3. **STUDY:** Who is acting in this passage? What things are involved? What ideas are present?

4. **STUDY:** What's going on in this verse? What action words do I see?

5.

CONNECT: How do the actions in this verse connect with the people or things involved?

Bonus Cross Reference

6.

LIVE IT: What is God saying to *me* in this verse? What does this passage speak to my life right now?

7.

PRAY: How do I want God to work in me through this study?

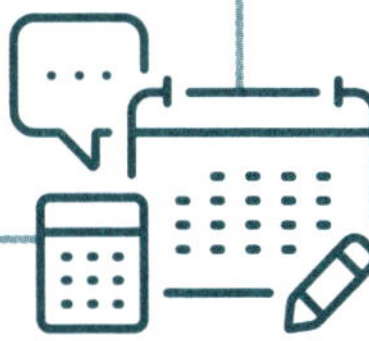

DATE:

1.

VERSE: What scripture am I exploring today?

In my favorite translation:

In another translation:

2.

NOTICE: What key words or themes immediately grab my attention? What questions come to mind?

Bonus Word Study

3.

STUDY: Who is acting in this passage? What things are involved? What ideas are present?

4.

STUDY: What's going on in this verse? What action words do I see?

5.

CONNECT: How do the actions in this verse connect with the people or things involved?

Bonus Cross Reference

6.

LIVE IT: What is God saying to *me* in this verse? What does this passage speak to my life right now?

7.

PRAY: How do I want God to work in me through this study?

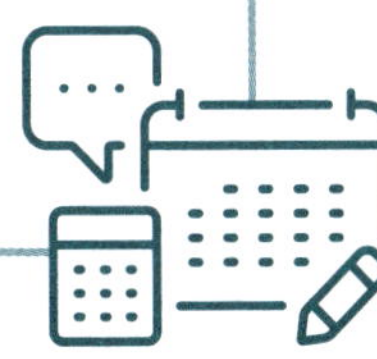

DATE:

1.

VERSE: What scripture am I exploring today?

In my favorite translation:

In another translation:

2.

NOTICE: What key words or themes immediately grab my attention? What questions come to mind?

Bonus Word Study

3.

STUDY: Who is acting in this passage? What things are involved? What ideas are present?

4.

STUDY: What's going on in this verse? What action words do I see?

5.

CONNECT: How do the actions in this verse connect with the people or things involved?

Bonus Cross Reference

6.

LIVE IT: What is God saying to *me* in this verse? What does this passage speak to my life right now?

7.

PRAY: How do I want God to work in me through this study?

DATE:

1.

VERSE: What scripture am I exploring today?

In my favorite translation:

In another translation:

2.

NOTICE: What key words or themes immediately grab my attention? What questions come to mind?

Bonus Word Study

3.

STUDY: Who is acting in this passage? What things are involved? What ideas are present?

4.

STUDY: What's going on in this verse? What action words do I see?

5.

CONNECT: How do the actions in this verse connect with the people or things involved?

Bonus Cross Reference

6.

LIVE IT: What is God saying to *me* in this verse? What does this passage speak to my life right now?

7.

PRAY: How do I want God to work in me through this study?

DATE:

1. **VERSE:** What scripture am I exploring today?

In my favorite translation:

In another translation:

2. **NOTICE:** What key words or themes immediately grab my attention? What questions come to mind?

Bonus Word Study

3. **STUDY:** Who is acting in this passage? What things are involved? What ideas are present?

4. **STUDY:** What's going on in this verse? What action words do I see?

5.

CONNECT: How do the actions in this verse connect with the people or things involved?

Bonus Cross Reference

6.

LIVE IT: What is God saying to *me* in this verse? What does this passage speak to my life right now?

7.

PRAY: How do I want God to work in me through this study?

DATE:

1\. **VERSE:** What scripture am I exploring today?

In my favorite translation:

In another translation:

2\. **NOTICE:** What key words or themes immediately grab my attention? What questions come to mind?

Bonus Word Study

3\. **STUDY:** Who is acting in this passage? What things are involved? What ideas are present?

4\. **STUDY:** What's going on in this verse? What action words do I see?

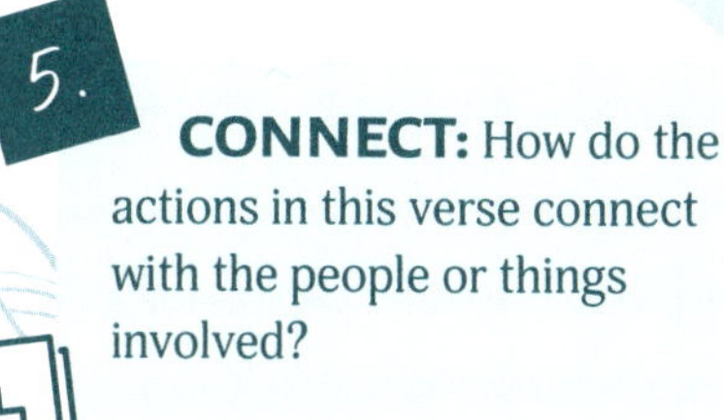

5.

CONNECT: How do the actions in this verse connect with the people or things involved?

Bonus Cross Reference

6.

LIVE IT: What is God saying to *me* in this verse? What does this passage speak to my life right now?

7.

PRAY: How do I want God to work in me through this study?

DATE:

1. **VERSE:** What scripture am I exploring today?

In my favorite translation:

In another translation:

2. **NOTICE:** What key words or themes immediately grab my attention? What questions come to mind?

Bonus Word Study

3. **STUDY:** Who is acting in this passage? What things are involved? What ideas are present?

4. **STUDY:** What's going on in this verse? What action words do I see?

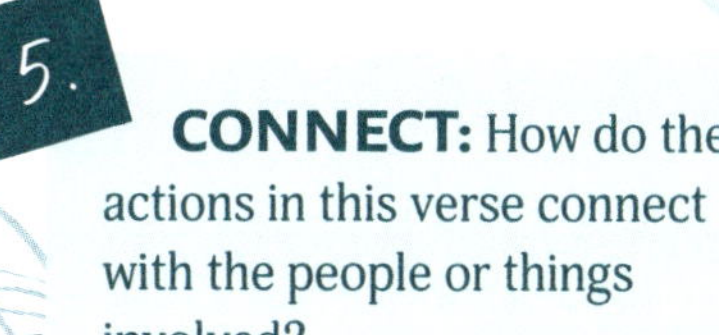

5.

CONNECT: How do the actions in this verse connect with the people or things involved?

Bonus Cross Reference

6.

LIVE IT: What is God saying to *me* in this verse? What does this passage speak to my life right now?

7.

PRAY: How do I want God to work in me through this study?

DATE:

1\.

VERSE: What scripture am I exploring today?

In my favorite translation:

In another translation:

2\.

NOTICE: What key words or themes immediately grab my attention? What questions come to mind?

Bonus Word Study

3\.

STUDY: Who is acting in this passage? What things are involved? What ideas are present?

4\.

STUDY: What's going on in this verse? What action words do I see?

5.

CONNECT: How do the actions in this verse connect with the people or things involved?

Bonus Cross Reference

6.

LIVE IT: What is God saying to *me* in this verse? What does this passage speak to my life right now?

7.

PRAY: How do I want God to work in me through this study?

DATE:

1. **VERSE:** What scripture am I exploring today?

In my favorite translation:

In another translation:

2. **NOTICE:** What key words or themes immediately grab my attention? What questions come to mind?

Bonus Word Study

3. **STUDY:** Who is acting in this passage? What things are involved? What ideas are present?

4. **STUDY:** What's going on in this verse? What action words do I see?

5.

CONNECT: How do the actions in this verse connect with the people or things involved?

Bonus Cross Reference

6.

LIVE IT: What is God saying to *me* in this verse? What does this passage speak to my life right now?

7.

PRAY: How do I want God to work in me through this study?

DATE:

1. **VERSE:** What scripture am I exploring today?

In my favorite translation:

In another translation:

2. **NOTICE:** What key words or themes immediately grab my attention? What questions come to mind?

Bonus Word Study

3. **STUDY:** Who is acting in this passage? What things are involved? What ideas are present?

4. **STUDY:** What's going on in this verse? What action words do I see?

5.

CONNECT: How do the actions in this verse connect with the people or things involved?

Bonus Cross Reference

6.

LIVE IT: What is God saying to *me* in this verse? What does this passage speak to my life right now?

7.

PRAY: How do I want God to work in me through this study?

DATE:

1.

VERSE: What scripture am I exploring today?

In my favorite translation:

In another translation:

2.

NOTICE: What key words or themes immediately grab my attention? What questions come to mind?

Bonus Word Study

3.

STUDY: Who is acting in this passage? What things are involved? What ideas are present?

4.

STUDY: What's going on in this verse? What action words do I see?

5.

CONNECT: How do the actions in this verse connect with the people or things involved?

Bonus Cross Reference

6.

LIVE IT: What is God saying to *me* in this verse? What does this passage speak to my life right now?

7.

PRAY: How do I want God to work in me through this study?

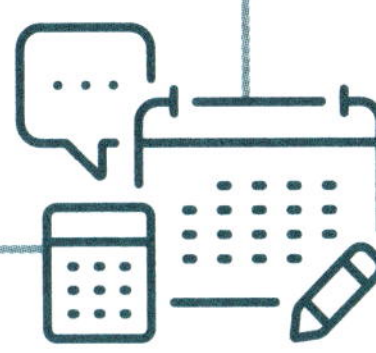

DATE:

1. **VERSE:** What scripture am I exploring today?

In my favorite translation:

In another translation:

2. **NOTICE:** What key words or themes immediately grab my attention? What questions come to mind?

Bonus Word Study

3. **STUDY:** Who is acting in this passage? What things are involved? What ideas are present?

4. **STUDY:** What's going on in this verse? What action words do I see?

5.

CONNECT: How do the actions in this verse connect with the people or things involved?

Bonus Cross Reference

6.

LIVE IT: What is God saying to *me* in this verse? What does this passage speak to my life right now?

7.

PRAY: How do I want God to work in me through this study?

DATE:

1. **VERSE:** What scripture am I exploring today?

In my favorite translation:

In another translation:

2. **NOTICE:** What key words or themes immediately grab my attention? What questions come to mind?

Bonus Word Study

3. **STUDY:** Who is acting in this passage? What things are involved? What ideas are present?

4. **STUDY:** What's going on in this verse? What action words do I see?

5.

CONNECT: How do the actions in this verse connect with the people or things involved?

Bonus Cross Reference

6.

LIVE IT: What is God saying to *me* in this verse? What does this passage speak to my life right now?

7.

PRAY: How do I want God to work in me through this study?

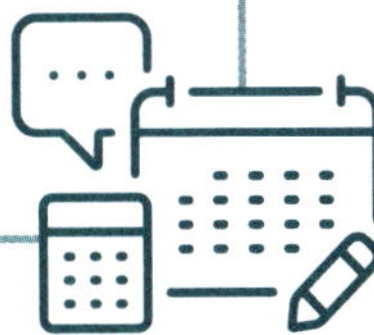

DATE:

1.

VERSE: What scripture am I exploring today?

In my favorite translation:

In another translation:

2.

NOTICE: What key words or themes immediately grab my attention? What questions come to mind?

Bonus Word Study

3.

STUDY: Who is acting in this passage? What things are involved? What ideas are present?

4.

STUDY: What's going on in this verse? What action words do I see?

5.

CONNECT: How do the actions in this verse connect with the people or things involved?

Bonus Cross Reference

6.

LIVE IT: What is God saying to *me* in this verse? What does this passage speak to my life right now?

7.

PRAY: How do I want God to work in me through this study?

DATE:

1. **VERSE:** What scripture am I exploring today?

In my favorite translation:

In another translation:

2. **NOTICE:** What key words or themes immediately grab my attention? What questions come to mind?

Bonus Word Study

3. **STUDY:** Who is acting in this passage? What things are involved? What ideas are present?

4. **STUDY:** What's going on in this verse? What action words do I see?

5.

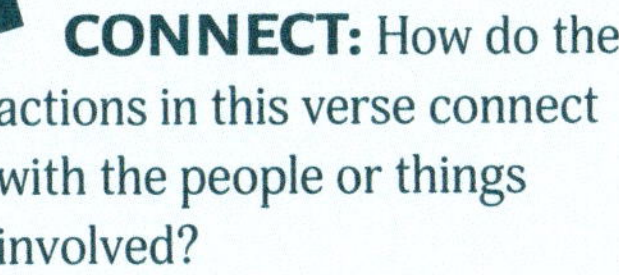

CONNECT: How do the actions in this verse connect with the people or things involved?

Bonus Cross Reference

6.

LIVE IT: What is God saying to *me* in this verse? What does this passage speak to my life right now?

7.

PRAY: How do I want God to work in me through this study?

DATE:

1.

VERSE: What scripture am I exploring today?

In my favorite translation:

In another translation:

2.

NOTICE: What key words or themes immediately grab my attention? What questions come to mind?

Bonus Word Study

3.

STUDY: Who is acting in this passage? What things are involved? What ideas are present?

4.

STUDY: What's going on in this verse? What action words do I see?

5.

CONNECT: How do the actions in this verse connect with the people or things involved?

Bonus Cross Reference

6.

LIVE IT: What is God saying to *me* in this verse? What does this passage speak to my life right now?

7.

PRAY: How do I want God to work in me through this study?

DATE:

1\. **VERSE:** What scripture am I exploring today?

In my favorite translation:

In another translation:

2\. **NOTICE:** What key words or themes immediately grab my attention? What questions come to mind?

Bonus Word Study

3\. **STUDY:** Who is acting in this passage? What things are involved? What ideas are present?

4\. **STUDY:** What's going on in this verse? What action words do I see?

5.

CONNECT: How do the actions in this verse connect with the people or things involved?

Bonus Cross Reference

6.

LIVE IT: What is God saying to *me* in this verse? What does this passage speak to my life right now?

7.

PRAY: How do I want God to work in me through this study?

DATE:

1.

VERSE: What scripture am I exploring today?

In my favorite translation:

In another translation:

2.

NOTICE: What key words or themes immediately grab my attention? What questions come to mind?

Bonus Word Study

3.

STUDY: Who is acting in this passage? What things are involved? What ideas are present?

4.

STUDY: What's going on in this verse? What action words do I see?

5.

CONNECT: How do the actions in this verse connect with the people or things involved?

Bonus Cross Reference

6.

LIVE IT: What is God saying to *me* in this verse? What does this passage speak to my life right now?

7.

PRAY: How do I want God to work in me through this study?

DATE:

1.

VERSE: What scripture am I exploring today?

In my favorite translation:

In another translation:

2.

NOTICE: What key words or themes immediately grab my attention? What questions come to mind?

Bonus Word Study

3.

STUDY: Who is acting in this passage? What things are involved? What ideas are present?

4.

STUDY: What's going on in this verse? What action words do I see?

5.

CONNECT: How do the actions in this verse connect with the people or things involved?

Bonus Cross Reference

6.

LIVE IT: What is God saying to *me* in this verse? What does this passage speak to my life right now?

7.

PRAY: How do I want God to work in me through this study?

DATE:

1\. **VERSE:** What scripture am I exploring today?

In my favorite translation:

In another translation:

2\. **NOTICE:** What key words or themes immediately grab my attention? What questions come to mind?

Bonus Word Study

3\. **STUDY:** Who is acting in this passage? What things are involved? What ideas are present?

4\. **STUDY:** What's going on in this verse? What action words do I see?

5.

CONNECT: How do the actions in this verse connect with the people or things involved?

Bonus Cross Reference

6.

LIVE IT: What is God saying to *me* in this verse? What does this passage speak to my life right now?

7.

PRAY: How do I want God to work in me through this study?

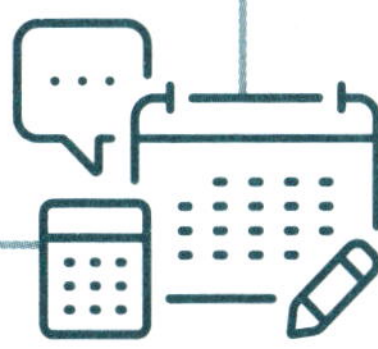

DATE:

1. **VERSE:** What scripture am I exploring today?

In my favorite translation:

In another translation:

2. **NOTICE:** What key words or themes immediately grab my attention? What questions come to mind?

Bonus Word Study

3. **STUDY:** Who is acting in this passage? What things are involved? What ideas are present?

4. **STUDY:** What's going on in this verse? What action words do I see?

5.

CONNECT: How do the actions in this verse connect with the people or things involved?

Bonus Cross Reference

6.

LIVE IT: What is God saying to *me* in this verse? What does this passage speak to my life right now?

7.

PRAY: How do I want God to work in me through this study?

DATE:

1\. **VERSE:** What scripture am I exploring today?

In my favorite translation:

In another translation:

2\. **NOTICE:** What key words or themes immediately grab my attention? What questions come to mind?

Bonus Word Study

3\. **STUDY:** Who is acting in this passage? What things are involved? What ideas are present?

4\. **STUDY:** What's going on in this verse? What action words do I see?

5.

CONNECT: How do the actions in this verse connect with the people or things involved?

Bonus Cross Reference

6.

LIVE IT: What is God saying to *me* in this verse? What does this passage speak to my life right now?

7.

PRAY: How do I want God to work in me through this study?

DATE:

1. **VERSE:** What scripture am I exploring today?

In my favorite translation:

In another translation:

2. **NOTICE:** What key words or themes immediately grab my attention? What questions come to mind?

Bonus Word Study

3. **STUDY:** Who is acting in this passage? What things are involved? What ideas are present?

4. **STUDY:** What's going on in this verse? What action words do I see?

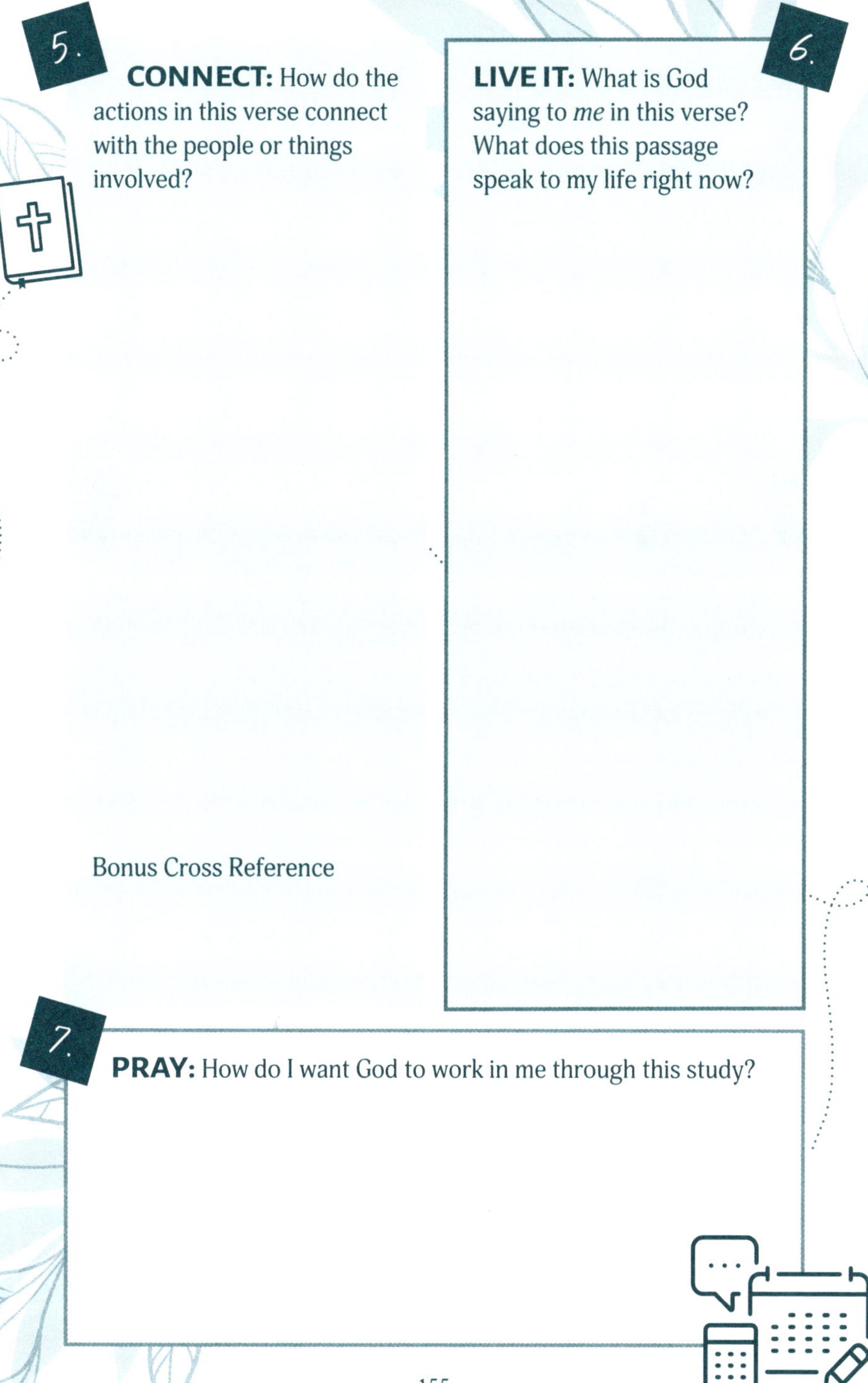

5.

CONNECT: How do the actions in this verse connect with the people or things involved?

Bonus Cross Reference

6.

LIVE IT: What is God saying to *me* in this verse? What does this passage speak to my life right now?

7.

PRAY: How do I want God to work in me through this study?

DATE:

1.

VERSE: What scripture am I exploring today?

In my favorite translation:

In another translation:

2.

NOTICE: What key words or themes immediately grab my attention? What questions come to mind?

Bonus Word Study

3.

STUDY: Who is acting in this passage? What things are involved? What ideas are present?

4.

STUDY: What's going on in this verse? What action words do I see?

5.

CONNECT: How do the actions in this verse connect with the people or things involved?

Bonus Cross Reference

6.

LIVE IT: What is God saying to *me* in this verse? What does this passage speak to my life right now?

7.

PRAY: How do I want God to work in me through this study?

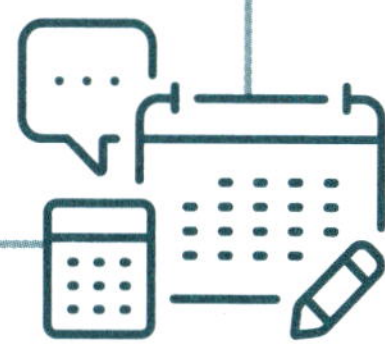

DATE:

1.

VERSE: What scripture am I exploring today?

In my favorite translation:

In another translation:

2.

NOTICE: What key words or themes immediately grab my attention? What questions come to mind?

Bonus Word Study

3.

STUDY: Who is acting in this passage? What things are involved? What ideas are present?

4.

STUDY: What's going on in this verse? What action words do I see?

5.

CONNECT: How do the actions in this verse connect with the people or things involved?

Bonus Cross Reference

6.

LIVE IT: What is God saying to *me* in this verse? What does this passage speak to my life right now?

7.

PRAY: How do I want God to work in me through this study?

DATE:

1.

VERSE: What scripture am I exploring today?

In my favorite translation:

In another translation:

2.

NOTICE: What key words or themes immediately grab my attention? What questions come to mind?

Bonus Word Study

3.

STUDY: Who is acting in this passage? What things are involved? What ideas are present?

4.

STUDY: What's going on in this verse? What action words do I see?

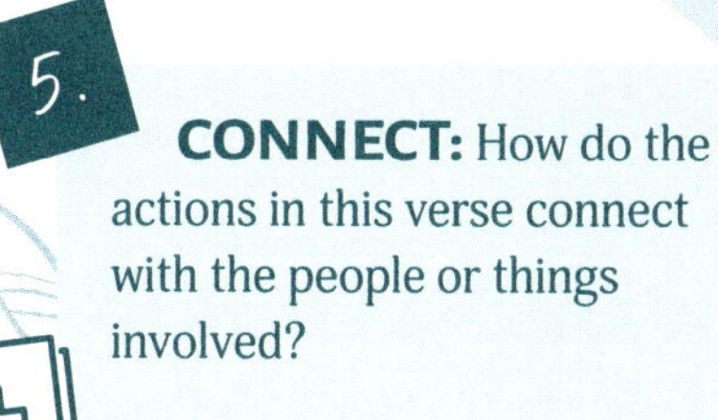

5.

CONNECT: How do the actions in this verse connect with the people or things involved?

Bonus Cross Reference

6.

LIVE IT: What is God saying to *me* in this verse? What does this passage speak to my life right now?

7.

PRAY: How do I want God to work in me through this study?

DATE:

1.

VERSE: What scripture am I exploring today?

In my favorite translation:

In another translation:

2.

NOTICE: What key words or themes immediately grab my attention? What questions come to mind?

Bonus Word Study

3.

STUDY: Who is acting in this passage? What things are involved? What ideas are present?

4.

STUDY: What's going on in this verse? What action words do I see?

5.

CONNECT: How do the actions in this verse connect with the people or things involved?

Bonus Cross Reference

6.

LIVE IT: What is God saying to *me* in this verse? What does this passage speak to my life right now?

7.

PRAY: How do I want God to work in me through this study?

DATE:

1. **VERSE:** What scripture am I exploring today?

In my favorite translation:

In another translation:

2. **NOTICE:** What key words or themes immediately grab my attention? What questions come to mind?

Bonus Word Study

3. **STUDY:** Who is acting in this passage? What things are involved? What ideas are present?

4. **STUDY:** What's going on in this verse? What action words do I see?

5.

CONNECT: How do the actions in this verse connect with the people or things involved?

Bonus Cross Reference

6.

LIVE IT: What is God saying to *me* in this verse? What does this passage speak to my life right now?

7.

PRAY: How do I want God to work in me through this study?

DATE:

1.

VERSE: What scripture am I exploring today?

In my favorite translation:

In another translation:

2.

NOTICE: What key words or themes immediately grab my attention? What questions come to mind?

Bonus Word Study

3.

STUDY: Who is acting in this passage? What things are involved? What ideas are present?

4.

STUDY: What's going on in this verse? What action words do I see?

5.

CONNECT: How do the actions in this verse connect with the people or things involved?

Bonus Cross Reference

6.

LIVE IT: What is God saying to *me* in this verse? What does this passage speak to my life right now?

7.

PRAY: How do I want God to work in me through this study?

DATE:

1.

VERSE: What scripture am I exploring today?

In my favorite translation:

In another translation:

2.

NOTICE: What key words or themes immediately grab my attention? What questions come to mind?

Bonus Word Study

3.

STUDY: Who is acting in this passage? What things are involved? What ideas are present?

4.

STUDY: What's going on in this verse? What action words do I see?

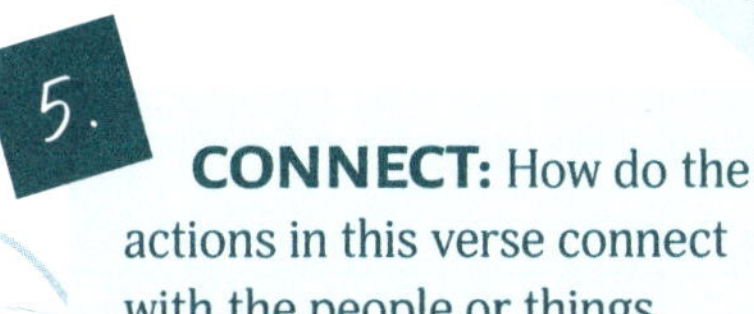

5.

CONNECT: How do the actions in this verse connect with the people or things involved?

Bonus Cross Reference

6.

LIVE IT: What is God saying to *me* in this verse? What does this passage speak to my life right now?

7.

PRAY: How do I want God to work in me through this study?

DATE:

1.

VERSE: What scripture am I exploring today?

In my favorite translation:

In another translation:

2.

NOTICE: What key words or themes immediately grab my attention? What questions come to mind?

Bonus Word Study

3.

STUDY: Who is acting in this passage? What things are involved? What ideas are present?

4.

STUDY: What's going on in this verse? What action words do I see?

5.

CONNECT: How do the actions in this verse connect with the people or things involved?

Bonus Cross Reference

6.

LIVE IT: What is God saying to *me* in this verse? What does this passage speak to my life right now?

7.

PRAY: How do I want God to work in me through this study?

DATE:

1. **VERSE:** What scripture am I exploring today?

In my favorite translation:

In another translation:

2. **NOTICE:** What key words or themes immediately grab my attention? What questions come to mind?

Bonus Word Study

3. **STUDY:** Who is acting in this passage? What things are involved? What ideas are present?

4. **STUDY:** What's going on in this verse? What action words do I see?

5.

CONNECT: How do the actions in this verse connect with the people or things involved?

Bonus Cross Reference

6.

LIVE IT: What is God saying to *me* in this verse? What does this passage speak to my life right now?

7.

PRAY: How do I want God to work in me through this study?

DATE:

1. **VERSE:** What scripture am I exploring today?

In my favorite translation:

In another translation:

2. **NOTICE:** What key words or themes immediately grab my attention? What questions come to mind?

Bonus Word Study

3. **STUDY:** Who is acting in this passage? What things are involved? What ideas are present?

4. **STUDY:** What's going on in this verse? What action words do I see?

5.

CONNECT: How do the actions in this verse connect with the people or things involved?

Bonus Cross Reference

6.

LIVE IT: What is God saying to *me* in this verse? What does this passage speak to my life right now?

7.

PRAY: How do I want God to work in me through this study?

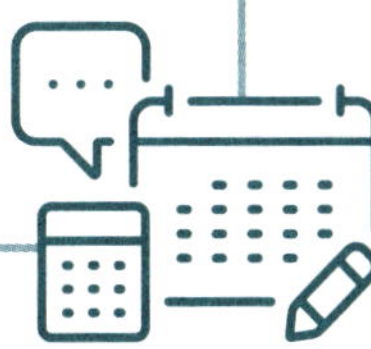

DATE:

1\. **VERSE:** What scripture am I exploring today?

In my favorite translation:

In another translation:

2\. **NOTICE:** What key words or themes immediately grab my attention? What questions come to mind?

Bonus Word Study

3\. **STUDY:** Who is acting in this passage? What things are involved? What ideas are present?

4\. **STUDY:** What's going on in this verse? What action words do I see?

5.

CONNECT: How do the actions in this verse connect with the people or things involved?

Bonus Cross Reference

6.

LIVE IT: What is God saying to *me* in this verse? What does this passage speak to my life right now?

7.

PRAY: How do I want God to work in me through this study?

DATE:

1.

VERSE: What scripture am I exploring today?

In my favorite translation:

In another translation:

2.

NOTICE: What key words or themes immediately grab my attention? What questions come to mind?

Bonus Word Study

3.

STUDY: Who is acting in this passage? What things are involved? What ideas are present?

4.

STUDY: What's going on in this verse? What action words do I see?

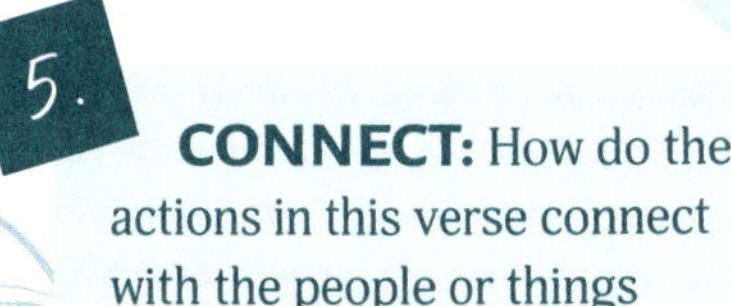

CONNECT: How do the actions in this verse connect with the people or things involved?

Bonus Cross Reference

6.

LIVE IT: What is God saying to *me* in this verse? What does this passage speak to my life right now?

7.

PRAY: How do I want God to work in me through this study?

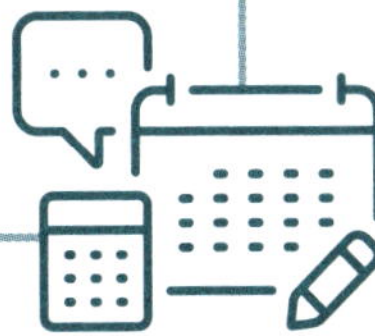

DATE:

1. **VERSE:** What scripture am I exploring today?

In my favorite translation:

In another translation:

2. **NOTICE:** What key words or themes immediately grab my attention? What questions come to mind?

Bonus Word Study

3. **STUDY:** Who is acting in this passage? What things are involved? What ideas are present?

4. **STUDY:** What's going on in this verse? What action words do I see?

5.

CONNECT: How do the actions in this verse connect with the people or things involved?

Bonus Cross Reference

6.

LIVE IT: What is God saying to *me* in this verse? What does this passage speak to my life right now?

7.

PRAY: How do I want God to work in me through this study?

DATE:

1. **VERSE:** What scripture am I exploring today?

In my favorite translation:

In another translation:

2. **NOTICE:** What key words or themes immediately grab my attention? What questions come to mind?

Bonus Word Study

3. **STUDY:** Who is acting in this passage? What things are involved? What ideas are present?

4. **STUDY:** What's going on in this verse? What action words do I see?

5.

CONNECT: How do the actions in this verse connect with the people or things involved?

Bonus Cross Reference

6.

LIVE IT: What is God saying to *me* in this verse? What does this passage speak to my life right now?

7.

PRAY: How do I want God to work in me through this study?

DATE:

1.

VERSE: What scripture am I exploring today?

In my favorite translation:

In another translation:

2.

NOTICE: What key words or themes immediately grab my attention? What questions come to mind?

Bonus Word Study

3.

STUDY: Who is acting in this passage? What things are involved? What ideas are present?

4.

STUDY: What's going on in this verse? What action words do I see?

5.

CONNECT: How do the actions in this verse connect with the people or things involved?

Bonus Cross Reference

6.

LIVE IT: What is God saying to *me* in this verse? What does this passage speak to my life right now?

7.

PRAY: How do I want God to work in me through this study?

DATE:

1. **VERSE:** What scripture am I exploring today?

In my favorite translation:

In another translation:

2. **NOTICE:** What key words or themes immediately grab my attention? What questions come to mind?

Bonus Word Study

3. **STUDY:** Who is acting in this passage? What things are involved? What ideas are present?

4. **STUDY:** What's going on in this verse? What action words do I see?

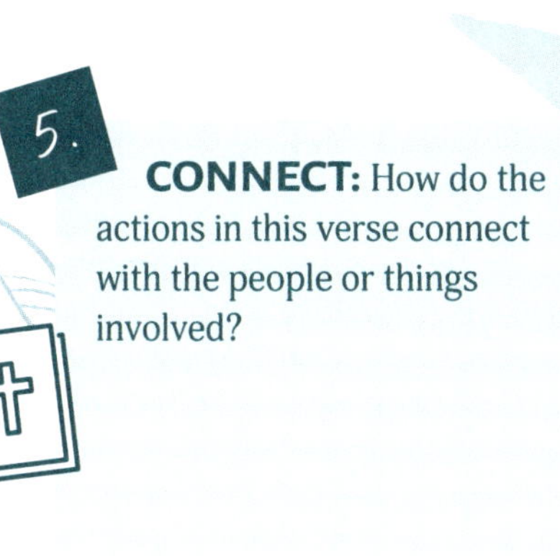

5.

CONNECT: How do the actions in this verse connect with the people or things involved?

Bonus Cross Reference

6.

LIVE IT: What is God saying to *me* in this verse? What does this passage speak to my life right now?

7.

PRAY: How do I want God to work in me through this study?

DATE:

1\.

VERSE: What scripture am I exploring today?

In my favorite translation:

In another translation:

2\.

NOTICE: What key words or themes immediately grab my attention? What questions come to mind?

Bonus Word Study

3\.

STUDY: Who is acting in this passage? What things are involved? What ideas are present?

4\.

STUDY: What's going on in this verse? What action words do I see?

5.

CONNECT: How do the actions in this verse connect with the people or things involved?

Bonus Cross Reference

6.

LIVE IT: What is God saying to *me* in this verse? What does this passage speak to my life right now?

7.

PRAY: How do I want God to work in me through this study?

DATE:

1.

VERSE: What scripture am I exploring today?

In my favorite translation:

In another translation:

2.

NOTICE: What key words or themes immediately grab my attention? What questions come to mind?

Bonus Word Study

3.

STUDY: Who is acting in this passage? What things are involved? What ideas are present?

4.

STUDY: What's going on in this verse? What action words do I see?

5.

CONNECT: How do the actions in this verse connect with the people or things involved?

Bonus Cross Reference

6.

LIVE IT: What is God saying to *me* in this verse? What does this passage speak to my life right now?

7.

PRAY: How do I want God to work in me through this study?